# ETHIOPIA

## Andrew Campbell

A+

**Smart Apple Media**

This book has been published in cooperation with Franklin Watts.

**Designer** Rita Storey
**Editor** Sarah Ridley
**Art Director** Jonathan Hair
**Editor-in-Chief** John C. Miles
**Picture Research** Diana Morris

**Picture credits**

Action Press/Rex Features: front cover tr.
Matti Bjorkman/Rex Features: front cover b, 27.
Pep Bonet/Panos: 23. Neil Cooper/Still Pictures: 14. Mark Edwards/Still Pictures: 12.
Empics/Topfoto: 16. Victor Englebert/Photographers Direct: 5.
Indrias Getachew/UNICEF: 25. Frances Linzee Gordon/Lonely Planet Images: 6.
Crispin Hughes/Panos: 19. Crispin Hughes/Still Pictures: 18.
Patricia Jordan/Still Pictures: 8. Knut Mueller/Still Pictures: 20.
K. Nomachi/Rex Features: 26. Picturepoint/Topfoto: 15.
Karel Prinsloo/AP/Empics: 11. Reuters/Corbis: 21.
Sipa Press/Rex Features: front cover tl, 13. Sven Torfinn/Panos: 24.
Peter Turnley/Corbis: 1, 9. Petterik Wiggers/Panos: 10.
Richard Young/Rex Features: 17.

Published in the United States by Smart Apple Media
2140 Howard Drive West, North Mankato, Minnesota 56003

Library of Congress Cataloging-in-Publication Data

Campbell, Andrew.
Ethiopia / by Andrew Campbell.
p. cm.—(Countries in the news)
Includes index.
ISBN-13: 978-1-59920-016-3
1. Ethiopia—Juvenile literature. I. Title.

DT373.C26 2007
963—dc22            2006027524

9 8 7 6 5 4 3 2 1

# CONTENTS

**YEARS OF TV AND NEWSPAPER REPORTS** *have led many people in the West to associate Ethiopia with famine and nothing more. While it is certainly one of the poorest countries in the world, Ethiopia is also one of the oldest, with a rich history, diverse landscapes, and a great number of different peoples and cultures.*

## HIGHS AND LOWS

Lying in the part of eastern Africa known as the Horn of Africa, Ethiopia is about twice the size of Texas. Stretching from the north to the center are the Ethiopian Highlands, an area of mountains, grasslands, and rivers. Farther south, the land becomes much flatter. This region is home to part of eastern Africa's massive Rift Valley, as well as the Danakil Depression, one of the lowest places on Earth. Here, temperatures can reach as high as 120 °F (50 °C).

## ANCIENT TRADITIONS

The contrasting landscapes of Ethiopia are inhabited by people who have adapted to very different habitats and have developed their own unique cultures. There are 80 different ethnic groups in Ethiopia, each with its own language and traditions. Some of these traditions have endured for thousands of years, but in recent decades, government resettlement programs and environmental damage have begun to threaten these ways of life (see pages 8–9 and 12–13).

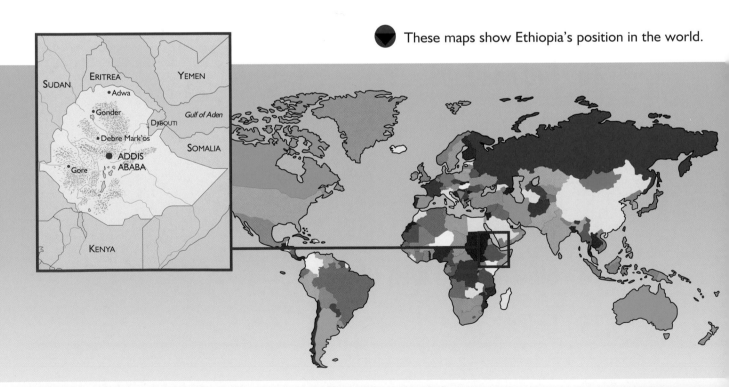

These maps show Ethiopia's position in the world.

Scientists take an underground water sample in the arid Danakil Depression area of Ethiopia.

## BIG ISSUES

Famine is, of course, one reason why Ethiopia is often in the news. The Live8 concerts of 2005 were inspired by the memory of Live Aid in 1985, organized to raise money to relieve the devastating Ethiopian famine of that year. War is another reason why the world's attention has focused on Ethiopia: a war with its neighbor, Eritrea, between 1998 and 2000 still causes problems today (see pages 20–21). Perhaps the biggest reason why Ethiopia hits the headlines is poverty. In 2005, it was estimated that an Ethiopian adult made, on average, $120 a year.

## KNOW YOUR FACTS

Here is some information about the countries bordering Ethiopia:

Sudan    Sudan's civil war, the longest-running in Africa, ended in 2005 after 21 years. A separate conflict in the Darfur region has created one and a half million refugees.

Uganda    Uganda has won praise for its economic growth and efforts to reduce HIV/AIDS infections. In the north, the government continues to fight a very violent uprising led by the Lord's Resistance Army, which began in the late 1980s.

Kenya    One of Ethiopia's most democratic neighbors, Kenya's two biggest problems are crime and corruption. Since 2005, western Kenya has experienced severe drought.

Somalia    Somalia has been without an effective government since the overthrow of its president in 1991. War, famine, and disease have killed up to a million people.

Djibouti    A small but very important country on the coast of the Red Sea, Djibouti lies between Africa and the Middle East. The United States has its only military base in Africa here.

Eritrea    Eritrea achieved independence from Ethiopia in 1993 but then went to war against Yemen and Ethiopia itself over its borders. These wars have left the Eritrean economy and people exhausted.

**ETHIOPIA IS ONE OF THE OLDEST COUNTRIES IN THE WORLD,** *with a history stretching back nearly 3,000 years. A major source of pride for Ethiopians is the fact that, while European powers colonized every other part of Africa in the 18th and 19th centuries, Ethiopia remained independent.*

## QUEENS AND KINGDOMS

Between 1000 and 400 B.C., the first civilization developed in Ethiopia, influenced by the Sabaean people of southern Arabia. According to the Bible, one of the rulers of Ethiopia, the Queen of Sheba, visited King Solomon of Israel and bore him a son—from whom later Ethiopian emperors claimed descent.

A much more powerful civilization emerged in the second century A.D. This was the kingdom of Aksum, based in present-day northern Ethiopia. Aksum became very wealthy through trade with other countries, but by the eighth century, it had lost its power.

## CHRISTIANITY AND ISLAM

Ethiopia's rulers and many of its people converted to Christianity in the fourth century A.D. After the spread of Islam, 400 years later, many other countries in Africa followed Arabia by converting to the religion preached by the Prophet Muhammad (c. 570–632). This left

● This statue in the Ethiopian capital Addis Ababa commemorates the rule of Haile Selassie (1930–74).

Ethiopia cut off from Christianity in Europe and set apart from its Muslim neighbors, who invaded the country between the 13th and 16th centuries to settle and spread their faith.

## HAILE SELASSIE

In the 19th and early 20th centuries, a series of strong emperors expanded Ethiopia's territory and turned it into a modern, centrally governed country. The last of these rulers was Haile Selassie, who became emperor in 1930 but had to escape to England during Italy's six-year conquest of his country (see panel, right). On his return, he incorporated Eritrea into Ethiopia, made his country a founding member of the United Nations, and developed its coffee industry (see pages 18–19). Some people, however, felt Ethiopia could only become truly modern by ending its system of emperor rule.

## DEMOCRACY VIA COMMUNISM

This thinking led to the overthrow of Haile Selassie in 1974 and his murder the next year. The military regime that replaced him, known as the Derg (meaning "committee"), slowly turned Ethiopia into a Communist country. The Derg received massive funding from the Soviet Union and transferred the ownership of all land from individuals to the state. But rebellions by different ethnic groups weakened the Derg's control, and in 1991, a new democratic government was formed under the leadership of Meles Zenawi, who became the country's prime minister.

## THE ITALIAN OCCUPATION

Ethiopia's first brush with Italy occurred in the late 19th century, when Italy—like France and Britain—was determined to develop an African empire. Italy gained control of the region around Ethiopia, establishing the colony of Eritrea in 1882. By the mid-1930s, Italy—now ruled by dictator Benito Mussolini—was determined to conquer Ethiopia. Economic developments set in place by Emperor Haile Selassie—such as Ethiopia's growing coffee industry—made the country all the more appealing to the Italian government.

Between late 1935 and mid-1936, the Italians gained control of the country, which joined Eritrea and Italian Somaliland to form Italian East Africa. More than 130,000 Italian workers were shipped over to build roads and houses in Ethiopia—particularly in the capital, Addis Ababa. When Italy joined World War II on the side of Hitler's Nazi Germany, Britain recognized Ethiopia as an ally. A joint British-Ethiopian force entered the country in January 1941; in a very short amount of time, the Italians had surrendered.

**THE LARGE NUMBER OF PEOPLE LIVING IN ETHIOPIA**—*estimated to be 73 million in 2005—makes it the third most populated country in Africa, after Nigeria and Egypt. This population is growing all the time: the UN believes it could be as high as 170 million by 2050.*

## DIFFERENT CULTURES

Ethiopia is home to many diverse peoples. The biggest ethnic group is the Oromo, who make up around 40 percent of the population. Oromo have Muslim, Christian, or traditional African beliefs, and most work as farmers or cattle breeders. The next largest groups are the Amhara and the Tigray, who live in the center and the north and hold Christian beliefs. Other groups include the southern-dwelling Gurage, the Harari—who live in the walled city of Harar in eastern Ethiopia—and the Karo, who paint their bodies in beautiful colors.

## NOMADS

Many ethnic groups in Ethiopia continue to live nomadic lifestyles, moving their herds of cattle, sheep, goats, or camels from one area of grazing land to another. These peoples include the Somali, the Afar, and the Borana. Today, the nomads' centuries-old way of life is threatened as more farmers move onto their traditional lands. The nomads believe that the government should protect their grazing territories and offer services such as mobile schools for their children. Some politicians, however, regard the nomadic way of life as old-fashioned and a block to the development of a modern economy.

## ETHNIC TENSIONS

Historically, all of the different peoples in Ethiopia were able to live quite peacefully together. Starting in the late 20th century, however, ethnic tension has become a sad fact of life. One reason for this is population growth, which has led more and more people to compete with each other for the same amount of land, food, and water.

 A Karo warrior, balancing a headrest on his shoulder. Karo men decorate themselves using clay, chalk, yellow mineral powder, iron ore, and charcoal to imitate the feathers of birds.

New arrivals to regions—either refugees escaping wars in other areas or countries, or people the government has resettled—have added to the unrest. In December 2003, for example, more than 400 people were killed in a single day in Gambela, in western Ethiopia. The fighting was caused by disagreements between the local Anyuak people and the Nuer population, which has risen sharply because of Nuer refugees fleeing the civil war in Sudan.

These Eritreans, displaced by war, have to live in a refugee camp in Ethiopia.

## GROUNDS FOR DEBATE

In order to reduce the risk of famine, the Ethiopian government has repeatedly resettled large numbers of people from dry, over-farmed areas to more fertile regions. Supporters of this policy argue that by doing this, the resettled people can make a better living from the land. Those against it say that the government's actions have disrupted communities and made civil unrest and ethnic tension more likely. What alternative solutions can you think of to moving people between regions?

**POLITICS IN ETHIOPIA IS VERY COMPLICATED,** *with more than 100 political parties in existence. Most of these parties represent different ethnic groups and struggle to make their voices heard.*

### MELES ZENAWI

The ruling political party, the Ethiopian People's Revolutionary Democratic Front (EPRDF), took power in 1991 and has held on to it ever since, winning three elections. To many people, its leader and prime minister, Meles Zenawi, is a hero for his role in overthrowing the Communist Derg government (see page 7), and he has won praise from Europe and the U.S. for developing Ethiopia's economy and promoting peace in Sudan and Somalia. Others argue that Zenawi is not the forward-thinking leader he claims to be. They point out that the Ethiopian government still owns all of the land in the country, a situation the EPRDF inherited from the Derg and refuses to change.

### MIXED RESULTS

The biggest challenge for Ethiopian politics is to ensure that all ethnic groups are fully represented. The EPRDF is dominated by Tigrayans, who make up between 5 and 10 percent of the country's population. Other people—particularly the Oromo, the largest ethnic group—think this is unfair. In the 1990s and 2000s, many have campaigned for the country to be divided into independent ethnic nations. Such campaigns can involve violence, such as bomb attacks on railroads and hotels.

### ELECTION NEWS— GOOD AND BAD

Land reform and ethnic representation were major issues during the 2005 general elections in Ethiopia. The good news about these

 This election protest in Addis Ababa in 2005 turned to tragedy when police shot protesters.

Ethiopians line up to vote in the 2005 elections, in which opposition parties gained popular support.

elections was the high turnout of voters (about 26 million had the right to vote, making it one of the biggest-ever elections in Africa) and the increasing activity of opposition parties, many of which had refused to take part in the elections of 1995 and 2000 because they mistrusted the government. The EPRDF won the 2005 election, but opposition parties gained more than 30 percent of the seats in the national parliament.

The bad news was that, as in the 1995 and 2000 elections, many people, including official observers, accused the EPRDF of using threats so that opposition candidates would not run in the elections and voters would feel scared to vote for any other party. The accusations led to an antigovernment protest in Addis Ababa, during which the police shot and killed 42 people.

**NEARLY EVERY YEAR ETHIOPIA MAKES HEADLINES** *around the world because of its food shortages. In 2003, the worst famine in two decades loomed in Ethiopia—more than 13 million people simply did not have enough food to eat. It was only through international aid (see pages 16–17) that a huge disaster was avoided.*

## UNRELIABLE NATURE

Some of the factors that lead to famine in Ethiopia, as in other African countries such as Niger and Sudan, are natural ones. Farmers in Ethiopia's dry lowlands

## KNOW YOUR FACTS

Ethiopia's 1984–85 famine, in which about one million people died, led to a huge international relief effort, the highlight of which was 1985's Live Aid concert. At the time, most people in the West put the famine down to drought; what they did not realize was the role that politics played. To begin with, Ethiopia's Communist government's policies of resettling people into villages and claiming all produce for the state meant that farmers could not grow enough food for themselves and local people. Then, when Western governments became aware of the crisis, they were slow to respond—none of them wanted to be seen supporting a Communist country. Finally, when food aid did arrive, there were reports that the government used it to feed its army.

irrigate their crops, but rain in this area can be very unreliable. For example, in 2003, both of the country's rainy seasons failed—the *meher*, the heavy summer rains, lasted one month instead of the usual three, while the *berg*, the short spring rains, did not come at all. Besides drought, another problem is locusts, which can eat an entire region's crops.

 Dust storms often blow away topsoil, causing devastation.

## HUMAN FACTORS

Other problems are human-made. They include poor farming practices, such as cutting down too many trees for firewood and overgrazing land with too many animals. These activities can result in soil erosion, so that even when it does rain, the ground is not able to absorb the moisture.

Other causes of famine include government policies such as the state ownership of land, which means that individual farmers own small areas of land that produce less than larger areas farmed by the same person. Many people suggest that the biggest cause of all is poverty: farmers are often too poor to buy proper seeds, tools, and fertilizers, and people are often too poor to buy food.

## MAKING CHANGES

In 2004, British journalist Michael Buerk went back to Ethiopia 20 years after reporting on its terrible famine of 1984–85. He concluded that little had changed for the better. Others argue that things have improved, but by nowhere near enough. Prime Minister Meles Zenawi, who comes from the famine-vulnerable region of Tigray, has made the fight against famine one of his most important goals. One thing his

An image of the 1984 famine. Pictures such as these prompted people around the world to give generously to relieve Ethiopia's distress.

government is doing is improving Ethiopia's road network, which is one of the worst in Africa. Road building is vital: in previous famines, the roads have been so bad or nonexistent that food grown in one part of the country could not be transported to another area where it was desperately needed.

NOT ONLY DO MANY ETHIOPIANS SUFFER *from a lack of water, but much of the water they do use puts their health at risk. Only 24 percent of the population has access to safe water—one of the lowest levels of any country in the world—while just 15 percent has adequate sanitation (the removal of sewage and garbage).*

## DISEASES

Unclean water and poor waste disposal provide a breeding ground for many diseases. These include malaria, a life-threatening condition carried by mosquitoes (which lay their eggs in water), the skin disease scabies, and trachoma, a type of eye infection.

Diarrhea is another illness caused by dirty water—for people in the West this is usually just a nuisance, but in poor countries, it can be a killer. One report says that 46 percent of deaths among Ethiopia's children under five are caused by diarrhea.

## SHORTAGES

One reason for poor levels of hygiene is simply water shortages, which force people to drink from still, sometimes stagnant pools and to be very sparing with their use of water. This can mean, for example, washing clothes less than once a month, even if they are very dirty, and drinking water that may have mud or worms in it. Another reason for poor hygiene is the lack of access to safe toilets. In the capital, Addis Ababa, more than a quarter of the three million inhabitants use streams running through their housing areas as toilets.

 This open sewer runs through a slum area of Addis Ababa.

## WORKING TOGETHER

Much needs to be done to improve this situation, and local communities and nongovernmental organizations (NGOs) are working hard. The British-based charity WaterAid, for example, brings technical expertise and equipment to help people access fresh water from springs and wells. In the Hitosa region of central Ethiopia, WaterAid has worked with around 60,000 local people to build a massive new water supply system.

## CLEANING UP

In the Tekle Haymonot district of Addis Ababa, locals are working to improve their sanitation levels in a different way. Each morning, people collect garbage from houses in the district—garbage that otherwise would have been left in the streets. Each household pays a small charge for this service and is responsible for keeping the area outside its front door clean. The result has been a big improvement in the health of residents.

## KNOW YOUR FACTS

Water shortages mean that Ethiopians, usually women, often have to walk long distances to fetch and carry supplies. Birkenesh Belete explains what life was like in her home of Boloso Sore, in southwest Ethiopia, before the charity Oxfam installed a water pump in her village: "We couldn't go twice to the river to fill and carry our pots, as we had to leave at 4 A.M. and didn't get back until 11 A.M. Then we had a lot of work to do. We had stomach problems, and our backs ached. We had problems in the pelvic area. Our legs ached from walking. We got headaches from getting up early and not getting enough sleep."

This young girl walks many miles to fetch fresh water in the jar on her back.

**DEVELOPMENT MEANS ANY ASSISTANCE** *from rich countries that helps poor nations become wealthier, more stable, and ultimately more able to cope without outside support. Development is a crucial issue in Ethiopia, where life expectancy is, on average, 48 years (compared to 78 years in the U.S.).*

## AID

In 2005, the Make Poverty History campaign, which brought together many international charities and NGOs, addressed the three types of development support that countries like Ethiopia need: aid, debt relief, and trade justice. Aid comes in many different forms. One form is emergency aid, which governments and NGOs send in response to crises such as Ethiopia's 2003 famine. This assistance is vital but often takes months to reach the neediest places. Many argue that long-term aid, such as providing farmers with better seeds and tools, is more beneficial.

## DEBT RELIEF

Debt relief is another way to help Ethiopia build its economy. Like other African countries, Ethiopia has borrowed a lot of money from Western banks and governments since the 1970s.

● The G8 world leaders met at Gleneagles, Scotland, in July 2005.

# GROUNDS FOR DEBATE

Supporters of trade barriers—mainly the richer nations that benefit from them—say that the restrictions protect jobs and industries in their countries. But poor nations counter that trade barriers make it difficult for them to sell their goods and earn money to lift themselves out of poverty. What do you think?

by making trade fair. This means that Western governments should stop the subsidies (payments) they give their own farmers to produce more food than is needed—a system that was first set up in Europe after World War II to prevent a repeat of wartime food shortages. It also means that Western countries should remove the barriers that prevent producers in poor countries from selling their goods to richer nations.

● Bob Geldof (left), with Paul McCartney (right), organized the Live8 concerts in 2005 to focus the world's attention on poverty and debt relief.

Because interest rates have risen very quickly during this period, much of the money Ethiopia paid back simply covered this increase and did not reduce the original debt. In 2002, for example, Ethiopia spent more money on its debts than on healthcare or education. In July 2005, however, leaders of the world's 8 richest countries—the G8—met in Scotland and agreed to cancel the debts of 18 of the world's poorest nations, including Ethiopia. This is a huge step forward, but some people are worried that rich countries will still recover the money owed to them by reducing the amount of aid they give.

## TRADE JUSTICE
Many Make Poverty History activists, along with many Ethiopians, argue that there is only one way to really help poor countries stand on their own two feet—

# THE COFFEE INDUSTRY

**COFFEE GROWING IS ETHIOPIA'S MOST IMPORTANT INDUSTRY** *and source of income. Around 15 million Ethiopians are involved in the coffee trade, either as farmers or processors, and about 35 percent of the money Ethiopia earns from selling goods to other countries comes from coffee.*

## COFFEE TALES

Ethiopia is the birthplace of coffee. According to Ethiopian history, coffee was discovered in about A.D. 1000, when a goat herder in Choche, in western Ethiopia, noticed that his goats made a lot of noise and refused to sleep after eating some strange berries. The goat herder tried the berries himself and found that he was no longer tired. Today, coffee plays a large part in Ethiopian culture.

● Coffee cherries are the ripe fruit of the coffee bush.

Visitors to a home will often wait while the host roasts coffee beans and brews and serves coffee in tiny cups. It is traditional for a guest to be served at least three cups.

## PRICE SLUMP

Since the late 1990s, Ethiopia's coffee farmers have faced a very difficult situation. Brazil and Vietnam both increased the amount of cheap coffee they produced, and as a result, there

## KNOW YOUR FACTS

Coffee is the second most valuable product in the world, after oil; people around the world drink about two and a half billion cups of coffee every day. The two most widely grown varieties of coffee are arabica, which is mild in flavor, and the stronger-tasting robusta. Arabica is the main coffee grown in Ethiopia.

After coffee cherries are harvested, they go to warehouses for sorting, pulping, fermenting, washing, and drying. The coffee beans are then bagged and shipped to Western countries for roasting and blending. Ethiopian farmers receive, on average, two percent of the price we pay for a jar or cup of coffee. The roaster (usually a big multinational company) receives an average of 64 percent, and the retailer 25 percent.

Farmers harvest coffee cherries between late September and December.

was simply too much coffee on the world market, and prices collapsed. In the mid-1990s, farmers in Choche, for example, sold their coffee for the equivalent of about $1.80 per pound (0.5 kg). By the early 2000s, this had dropped to $0.20 or less for the same amount. Many farmers could not afford to buy adequate food or to send their children to school.

## TOO MUCH CHAT

Many farmers began to replace their coffee crops with chat, a plant whose leaves are chewed or boiled as a mild drug. Chat is popular in Ethiopia, so at least farmers can earn money this way. However, growing it involves clearing the acacias and other trees under which coffee bushes grow, which can damage the local environment.

## COFFEE COOPERATIVES

Another way coffee farmers can protect their interests is to join a coffee cooperative. Many farmers sell their beans to traders, who sell them to exporters, who, in turn, sell them to foreign buyers—from Nestlé to Starbucks. Cooperatives, on the other hand, buy from the farmer and sell directly to international buyers, including Fairtrade coffee companies, which pay farmers more and so charge customers more in return. Cooperatives share any profits they make with farmers; they also help them transport and store their beans, offer loans for new equipment, and educate farmers about the world coffee market and changing international tastes.

**FROM 1998 TO 2000, A WAR BETWEEN ETHIOPIA** *and its northern neighbor Eritrea killed as many as 75,000 people and forced more than 350,000 to flee their homes. Today, the aftermath of the war continues to affect many people on both sides.*

## FROM FRIENDS TO ENEMIES

Eritrea became part of Ethiopia in 1962, but following the overthrow of Ethiopia's Communist government in 1991, it became independent in 1993. Relations between the two countries were good at this time: Ethiopia's prime minister Meles Zenawi and Eritrea's president Isaias Afewerki were friends who had fought alongside each other against the Communist regime. In May 1998, however, Eritrea moved soldiers into the region of Badme on Ethiopia's north western border. When Eritrea refused to withdraw, Ethiopia declared war.

## WAR AND UNEASY PEACE

Both sides assembled around 300,000 soldiers along the border, while their air forces bombed each other's airports and towns. Ethiopia forced thousands of Eritreans living inside its border north into Eritrea; Eritrea responded by expelling thousands of Ethiopians. The violence and refugee crisis continued until June 2000, when both governments called a ceasefire. They agreed to set up an independent boundary commission, made up of lawyers who would decide how the border between the two nations should be fixed. In 2003, the commission decided on a new border—changes included giving Badme to Eritrea. The Ethiopian government has refused to accept this decision, and tension between both sides rumbles on.

## THE HUMAN COST

People on both sides of the Ethiopian-Eritrean border continue to suffer because of the war. Many still live in refugee camps, and others are at risk from land mines planted along the border during the war. Between 1998 and 2003, 550 land mine explosions injured or killed civilians—and these were just the incidents that were reported.

Starving Eritrean refugees await grain distribution from the World Food Program.

The costs of war have been huge for both countries. Ethiopia spent hundreds of millions of dollars on the conflict, which also caused many foreign businesses to stop investing in the country. All of this is money that Ethiopia desperately needs. Another effect of the war has been to reduce Ethiopia's access to the sea. Previously, it relied on Eritrea's ports of Assab and Massawi to send and receive goods by ship; now, businesses have to use the port of Djibouti, a small country to the northeast.

 An Eritrean soldier keeps guard near the border with Ethiopia.

## KNOW YOUR FACTS

The dispute over the 560–mile (900 km) border between Ethiopia and Eritrea is a matter of national pride. Eritrea argues that the border should reflect the one set by Italy in 1902, while Ethiopia wants the border to be where it was before Eritrea's invasion in 1998. During the 1980s, Ethiopian Tigrayans, rebelling against their Communist government, expanded their control into Eritrean territory. Since they then became the dominant group in Ethiopia's new government, this territory has remained part of Ethiopia.

# 10 HIV AND AIDS

ETHIOPIA HAS ONE OF THE LARGEST NUMBERS of people affected with HIV or AIDS. Other African nations have higher percentages of people infected, but around one and a half million people live with HIV or AIDS in Ethiopia, posing a great challenge to individuals and the government.

## YOUTH AT RISK

More than 25 percent of Ethiopia's population is under 25 years old, and the number of young people with HIV or AIDS is very high. In 2004, UNAIDS (the UN's AIDS program) estimated that about 96,000 Ethiopian children under 15 had HIV. There are many reasons why HIV infections occur in Ethiopia, from cultural barriers about condom use to a lack of information about how to avoid infection.

## GET THE MESSAGE

Education is therefore crucial in spreading awareness about HIV and AIDS to ordinary Ethiopians. Peer education—young people teaching other young people—is a powerful way to get the message across and is actively encouraged by the government. One peer education group is the Tabor-Wegagen Anti-AIDS Association, which was set up by a group of young people. Members of the association teach teenagers about HIV and AIDS for a period of two months. They also write and perform plays on AIDS topics.

## AIDS AND CHILDREN

There are as many as 1.2 million AIDS orphans in Ethiopia—children whose parents have died from the disease. On October 25, 2005, Richard Mabala, the head of UNICEF's Youth, Protection, and HIV/AIDS program in Ethiopia, spoke about their situation:

"The Global Campaign being launched today talks about children as the Missing Face of AIDS. Maybe we could talk about the missing faces, or even the invisible faces. Instead, the faces have been turned into staggering statistics, huge numbers that we throw around in our speeches, xxx infected every minute, yyy orphans, zzz numbers of children needing treatment, etc. And as we stand and pronounce the statistics, they continue to get bigger so that our next speech will have to revise the statistics up once again. And because the statistics are so big, just like a Hurricane Katrina or a tsunami or an earthquake, they can actually disempower us as we are overcome by a sense of helplessness. How can we ever hope to deal with such a situation? Where do we start? How can we find the resources? And yet each one of these statistics dreams, just like you and I dream. In our case, our dreams inspire us to action."

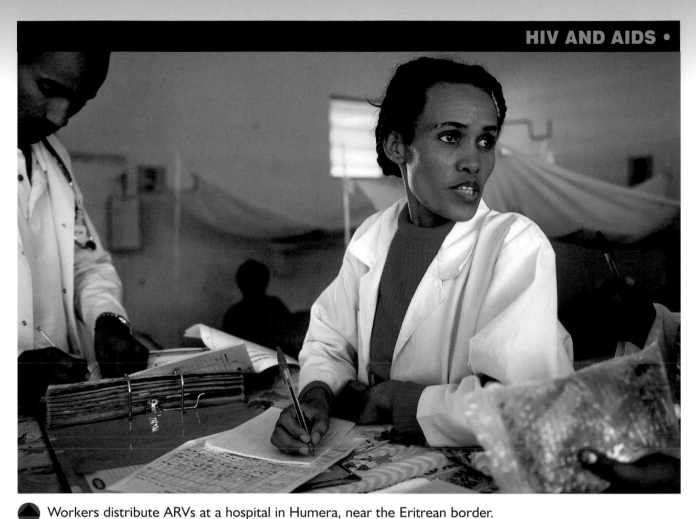

▲ Workers distribute ARVs at a hospital in Humera, near the Eritrean border.

## WHAT PRICE A LIFE?

The real issue for those who have HIV or AIDS, however, is gaining access to drugs called antiretrovirals (ARVs). ARVs can help HIV-infected people live healthy lives and have led to a dramatic reduction in AIDS-related deaths in the West. But most people in Ethiopia, as in the rest of Africa, cannot afford the cost of ARV treatment. In 2004, UNAIDS estimated that 245,000 Ethiopians needed ARVs but pointed out that only 13,100 people were actually taking them. The World Health Organization has led a campaign to massively increase the number of people on ARVs in Ethiopia, but progress has been slow.

## GROUNDS FOR DEBATE

One reason why ARVs are not as widely available as they could be is that drug companies refuse to allow "generic" drug manufacturers to make cheap copies of their medicines. The drug companies say that in a free market, the right to profit from the sale of their product should be protected. Opponents say that the drug companies should be forced to allow cheap copies to be made to deal with the HIV/AIDS humanitarian emergency. What do you think?

**IT IS NOT EASY GROWING UP IN ETHIOPIA.** *As many as half a million children die each year from diseases and malnutrition. For those who survive, childhood can be cut short by early marriage or the need to work to support families.*

### EARLY MARRIAGE

Getting married at an early age—as young as eight or nine—is common in Ethiopia. According to government figures, 57 percent of girls marry before the age of 18, while in some regions (such as Amhara and Tigray), this can be around 80 percent. Arranged marriages are a major way of securing alliances between families. In addition, because life expectancy is low, parents have an extra desire to see their children married and settled as quickly as possible—unmarried girls and women risk being seen as outcasts in Ethiopian society.

### CHILD LABOR

Boys can get married at an early age, too, although this is more common for girls, who as wives are expected to cook, clean, collect firewood and water, and help with farming tasks. Boys will often assist their fathers by tending cattle, planting seeds, looking after crops, and helping to harvest them. This pattern of

Children and teenagers gather outside a school in Tsiska, near Lalibela.

family responsibility and farming duties is repeated across Ethiopia, where the vast majority of people live in the countryside.

## SCHOOL PROBLEMS

According to UNICEF, about 7 out of 10 Ethiopian children do not go to school at all, or fail to finish their primary education. Early marriage and child labor partly explain this situation; another reason is that schools are few and far between—children may have to walk long distances to get to school, and when they get there, classes can number more than 100 children. Another factor is poverty: parents have no money for school uniforms or books and need their children to stay at home and work.

## CHANGING ATTITUDES

Many people believe that changing parents' attitudes will help children have more access to education. Many Ethiopians have traditionally placed little value on girls' schooling, so teachers persuade parents that everyone has a right to education and that early marriage can harm young people's development.

One positive example has been set by Samia Sadik, a student from Dire Dawa in eastern Ethiopia. Samia refused to accept her parents' wishes and get married, a decision her schoolteachers supported her in making. Samia has now completed her secondary schooling and hopes to become a doctor.

Samia Sadik, now training to become a doctor.

## EDUCATION

Ethiopia's world champion runner, Berhane Adere, is an activist for increasing children's access to sports and education in her home country: "Education is important for every child because education is something that is above everything else. Being educated means having knowledge. Being educated allows you to eat, drink, and clothe yourself. You are able to understand things if you are educated. The country can grow if there is education. I believe that everyone needs to be educated."

**AS ETHIOPIA'S GOVERNMENT AND PEOPLE LOOK TO THE FUTURE,** *the need to develop the country's economy—to cope with a growing population, poverty, drought, and health problems—becomes more urgent. Tourism is seen by many as a possible solution, which could earn Ethiopia millions of vital dollars.*

### PLACES TO VISIT

Ethiopia certainly has lots of tourist potential. Attractions include Addis Ababa's open-air market, the Merkato, said to be the biggest in Africa; the stunning Simien mountains in the north; and the town of Lalibela, with its 11th- and 12th-century churches carved out of volcanic rock. Ethiopians are world-famous for their friendliness, and their customs and celebrations are fascinating to watch and take part in. The country is also home to rich plant and animal life, including 28 mammal species found nowhere else on Earth, such as the mountain nyala (a type of antelope) and the Ethiopian wolf.

### PROBLEMS TO FIX?

Some people argue that Ethiopia has a long way to go before it can seriously offer itself as a tourist destination on a large scale. Its road network is still very

Traditional dances—such as this one performed by the Hama people—attract tourists.

The recent success of Ethiopia's middle-distance runners is helping to change attitudes toward the country around the world.

limited, for example, and outside Addis Ababa there are few hotels that can meet the expectations of wealthy Western visitors. Others point out that roads and hotels are being built. A bigger issue might well be the country's image: many people in the West—unfairly—see Ethiopia in terms of famine and poverty, and not as a vacation destination.

### OTHER THINGS FIRST
Many people think Ethiopia needs to concentrate on other industries before tourism. Agriculture is by far the country's biggest earner, and for things to improve, farmers need to diversify their crops away from coffee and grow more grains, sugar, fruits, and vegetables. The energy industry is something else Ethiopia needs to develop, since many people still live without electricity. The government recognizes this. In 2004, it opened the country's biggest hydroelectric power plant at Gilgel-Gibe, near Addis Ababa.

**1000–400 B.C.** First civilization develops in Ethiopia.

**2ND CENTURY A.D.** Kingdom of Aksum established in present-day northern Ethiopia.

**4TH CENTURY** Introduction of Christianity to Ethiopia from Egypt.

**8TH CENTURY** Aksumite power collapses.

**1530–31** Muslim forces conquer much of Ethiopia.

**1818** Military leader Lij Kassa begins building up power in previously separate Ethiopian regions.

**1855** Lij Kassa becomes Emperor Tewodros II.

**1889** Emperor Menelik II, king of Shoa in central Ethiopia, takes the throne.

**1895** Italy invades Ethiopia. The Italians are defeated the next year but retain control of Eritrea.

**1916** Menelik II's daughter, Zawditu, comes to the throne but rules through her cousin, Ras Tafari Makonnen.

**1930** Ras Tafari is crowned Emperor Haile Selassie.

**1935** Italy invades Ethiopia for the second time. The Italians rule Ethiopia and Eritrea until 1941, when British and Ethiopian soldiers force them out.

**1962** Haile Selassie makes Eritrea part of Ethiopia.

**1972–74** Around 200,000 people die because of famine in north-central Ethiopia.

**1974** A military coup led by the Derg (committee) forces Haile Selassie from power.

**1977** Colonel Mengistu Haile Mariam becomes Ethiopia's leader.

**1977–78** Mengistu orders a campaign of intimidation against opponents of the Derg—thousands of people are killed.

**1984–85** Famine in Ethiopia kills up to one million people.

**1986** The country's first AIDS cases are reported.

**1989** The Tigrayan People's Liberation Front joins forces with other ethnic opposition movements to the Derg to become the Ethiopian People's Revolutionary Democratic Front (EPRDF).

**1991** EPRDF forces expel Mengistu from the country and take over power.

**1993** Eritrea becomes independent from Ethiopia.

**1994** A new constitution divides the country into nine regional states and two self-governing cities, Addis Ababa and Dire Dawa.

**1995** Ethiopia holds its first democratic elections; Meles Zenawi, the EPRDF leader, becomes prime minister.

**1998** Start of the two-year Ethiopia-Eritrea war.

**2000** The Ethiopian and Eritrean governments sign a peace agreement in Algeria.

**2000** Haile Selassie, murdered by the Derg in 1975, is finally buried in Addis Ababa's Trinity Cathedral.

**2000** Ethiopia's coffee industry crashes.

**2003** An independent boundary commission decides on the new border between Ethiopia and Eritrea. Ethiopia refuses to accept the decision.

**2004** The government begins a resettlement program to move more than two million from drought-affected regions.

**2005** The third general election since the overthrow of the Derg is held. There are claims of electoral fraud, and police shoot and kill 42 protestors.

**2005** G8 leaders agree to cancel all of Ethiopia's outstanding debts.

# BASIC FACTS

**LOCATION:** East Africa.

**TOTAL LAND AREA:** 437,600 square miles (1,133,380 sq km).

**POPULATION:** 73,053,286 (2005 estimate). Population growth rate: 2.36 percent (2005 estimate).

**MAJOR ETHNIC GROUPS:** Oromo, Amhara, Tigray, Sidamo, Shankella, Somali, Afar, Gurange.

**EMPLOYMENT AND INDUSTRIES:** Agriculture (85 percent of population), mining, chemicals.

**HIGHEST MOUNTAIN:** Ras Dashen (15,157 feet, or 4,620 m), the fourth-highest in Africa.

**MAJOR RIVERS:** The Blue Nile, the Awash, the Omo, the Wabe Shebele.

# GLOSSARY AND WEB SITES

**AIDS (Acquired Immune Deficiency Syndrome)**   A collection of infections and cancers that people with HIV can develop.

**Antiretrovirals (ARVs)**   Drugs that act against HIV by stopping it from making copies of itself inside white blood cells.

**Civil war**   A war between rival groups within a country. African history since the late 20th century is full of civil wars—Ethiopia is no exception.

**Communism**   A political and economic system in which the state owns all property. Individuals are provided with work, food, and housing.

**Ethnic group**   A group of people who are bound together by their race, language, traditions, or nation.

**Ethnic representation**   Standing up for the rights of individual ethnic groups. Many people think there should be more ethnic representation in Ethiopia since the government is dominated by one ethnic group.

**Famine**   An extreme and long-lasting food shortage, leading to malnutrition (a condition caused by eating poor or inadequate food), starvation, and possibly death.

**HIV (Human Immunodeficiency Virus)**   The virus that causes people to develop AIDS. Once someone is infected with HIV, it stays with them for life.

**Irrigation**   An artificial system that channels water through farmland to help farmers grow crops. Very little of Ethiopia's farmlands are currently irrigated.

**Land mine**   An explosive device buried in the ground. During war, soldiers bury land mines so that enemy troops or vehicles will tread on them, causing an explosion. After wars, however, unexploded landmines remain in the ground and can be set off by civilians—often children—and animals.

**Land reform**   Efforts to change the way land is owned. In Ethiopia, many demand land reform to end the state, or national, ownership of land, which dates back to the Communist period.

**Life expectancy**   The average age that a person can expect to live to. Life expectancy is much lower in Ethiopia than in Western countries.

**Nomad**   Someone with no fixed home who moves about a particular region or territory, usually with animals.

**Nongovernmental organizations (NGOs)**   Independent, not-for-profit organizations that campaign, provide a service, or help people.

**Refugees**   People who are forced to leave their homes because of war or political upheaval. Many escape to other countries where they apply for asylum (permission to remain).

**Resettlement program**   A government program to move large numbers of people from one region to another—in Ethiopia's case, away from drought-ridden or over-farmed areas to more fertile ones.

**Soil erosion** When soil that is not protected by plants blows away in the wind or is washed away by heavy rains. Cutting down trees and overgrazing are two causes of soil erosion.

**Soviet Union** Communist empire that consisted of Russia and much of eastern Europe and central Asia. It lasted from 1917 to 1991.

**UNICEF (United Nations Children's Fund)** An agency of the United Nations that runs development programs for children in developing countries.

**United Nations** The international organization established in 1945 to promote peace and cooperation between countries.

**World Health Organization** An agency of the United Nations, set up in 1948 to promote health and tackle disease around the world.

# USEFUL WEB SITES

**http://www.addistribune.com**
The online version of Ethiopia's English-language newspaper.

**http://www.ethiopialives.net**
In 2005, 19 Ethiopians from different parts of the country used digital cameras to record their lives and experiences.

**http://www.makepovertyhistory.org**
Learn more about the goals and achievements of this campaign.

**http://www.ethiopians.com**
Lots of information about Ethiopia.

**http://www.oxfam.org/en/programs/development/hafrica/ethiopia_irrigation**
Read about the development work Oxfam undertakes in Ethiopia.

**http://www.wateraid.org**
Find out about this charity that helps countries gain more access to clean water.

**http://www.unaids.org**
The Web site of UNAIDS features country profiles of the impact of HIV and AIDS.

**http://www.unicef.org/ethiopia**
The Web site of UNICEF in Ethiopia—learn about its role in helping to deal with poverty, health, and education issues.

**Note to parents and teachers:**
Every effort has been made to ensure that the Web sites in this book are suitable for children, that they are of the highest educational value, and that they contain no inappropriate or offensive material. However, because of the nature of the Internet, it is impossible to guarantee that the contents of these sites will not be altered. We strongly advise that Internet access be supervised by a responsible adult.